MASSAGE COUPONS
FOR HER

COPYRIGHT © 2021 NADINE DORIS SPARROW
ALL RIGHTS RESERVED

PRACTICAL TIPS

1. A SUITABLE PLACE

IN ORDER FOR YOUR PARTNER TO BE ABLE TO COMPLETELY RELAX, THE ENVIRONMENT HAS TO BE WELL PREPARED. YOU NEED TO MAKE SURE THAT THE WHOLE ROOM AND IN PARTICULAR A BED/TABLE ARE CLEAN. NEXT THING IS CANDLELIGHT. IT'S PRETTY IMPORTANT TO USE CANDLES INSTEAD OF ELECTRIC LIGHT BECAUSE ONLY NATURAL LIGHT CAN CREATE A SPECIFIC, RELAXING AND SENSUAL ATMOSPHERE. THE LAST THING YOU NEED TO REMEMBER IS SOFT, AMBIENT MUSIC.

2. A PROPER MASSAGE OIL

IT IS IMPORTANT TO USE ONLY NATURAL, CLEAR OIL. A GOOD IDEA IS TO ADD TO THE OIL JUST A FEW DROPS OF ESSENTIAL OIL TO ENHANCE THE AROMATIC EXPERIENCE. REMEMBER TO MAKE SURE THAT THE OIL IS COMFORTABLY WARM. TO WARM IT UP, PUT THE OIL ON YOUR HANDS AND RUB THEM TOGETHER VIGOROUSLY FOR A COUPLE OF SECONDS JUST BEFORE PUTTING THEM ON YOUR PARTNER SKIN.
BEFORE USING ESSENTIAL OILS ON A LARGE AREA OF SKIN, IT'S ALSO IMPORTANT TO DO A PATCH TEST TO SEE HOW YOUR SKIN WILL REACT. TO DO THAT APPLY A FEW DROPS OF DILUTED ESSENTIAL OIL ONTO A SMALL PATCH OF SKIN AND WAIT 24 HOURS, AFTER THAT CHECK IF YOU/YOUR PARTNER HAVE ANY SIGNS OF AN ALLERGIC REACTION.

3. COMMUNICATE WITH YOUR PARTNER

GENERALLY, DURING A MASSAGE, YOU SHOULD USE LIGHT, SMOOTH TOUCH. HOWEVER, YOU NEED TO CHECK FROM TIME TO TIME IF THE PRESSURE IS OKAY. YOU SHOULD KNOW THAT SOME PARTS OF OUR BODY ARE MORE SENSITIVE THAN OTHERS. YOUR PARTNER MAY PREFER YOU TO CHANGE THE PRESSURE DURING MASSAGE A PARTICULAR PART OF THE BODY. FIRST OF ALL, BEFORE YOU START, ASK IF ANY AREAS NEED MORE ATTENTION. IF YOU GET FAMILIAR WITH YOUR PARTNER'S NEEDS, YOU WILL BE MORE CONFIDENT THAT YOU ARE DOING A GOOD JOB AND YOUR PARTNER WILL BE MORE PLEASED.

HEAD MASSAGE

DO YOU SUFFER FROM HEADACHES? MAYBE YOU HAVE SOME STRESS PROBLEMS? A HEAD MASSAGE CAN HELP IN DEALING WITH THESE ISSUES. THIS TYPE OF MASSAGE IS VERY HELPFUL IN PROMOTING RELAXATION AND REDUCING STRESS. IT LOWERS BODY PRESSURE, REDUCES TENSION HEADACHE SYMPTOMS AND EVEN PROMOTES HAIR GROWTH. A HEAD MASSAGE TECHNIQUE FOCUSES ON DELIVERING SLOW, GENTLE STROKES ON YOUR HEAD AND WORK UP TO LIGHT CIRCULAR MOTIONS THAT GO ACROSS THE HEAD. ALTHOUGH YOU CAN DO A HEAD MASSAGE WITHOUT IT, I RECOMMENDED USING SOME ESSENTIAL OIL. YOU MAY LIKE THE AROMA AND ADDED BENEFITS OF USING THEM.

FOOT MASSAGE

THESE DAYS WE LIVE IN A HURRY, WE ARE ALWAYS BUSY, THAT'S WHY OUR FEET WORK HARD EVERY DAY. JUST LIKE A NECK, BACK, AND SHOULDERS, FEET CAN ALSO BENEFIT FROM REGULAR MASSAGE SESSIONS. IT CAN HELP SLEEP BETTER AND LEAVE YOU WITH REJUVENATED ENERGY TO BRING TO YOUR DAY. THESE BENEFITS ARE CONNECTED WITH THE BELIEF THAT APPLYING PRESSURE TO MORE THAN 7,000 NERVES IN A FOOT CAN RELEASE ENERGETIC BLOCKAGES IN THE REST OF A BODY. A FOOT MASSAGE IS ALSO VERY USEFUL IF WE WANT TO IMPROVE THE CIRCULATION OF BLOOD AROUND THE BODY. GENERALLY, FOOT MASSAGE SESSIONS ARE PERFORMED USING HANDS, BUT YOU CAN USE SOME EXTRA EQUIPMENT SUCH, AS STICKS OR ROLLERS.

SWEDISH MASSAGE

A SWEDISH MASSAGE IS ONE OF THE MOST POPULAR MASSAGE TECHNIQUE IN THE WESTERN WORLD.
AS THE NAME SUGGESTS, ORIGINALLY IT COMES FROM SWEDEN. IT INVOLVES USING A LOT OF FORCE TO RELIEVE PRESSURE AND PAIN. IT IS A WHOLE-BODY MASSAGE TECHNIQUE THAT HELPS IN RESTORING HEALTH - CREATING A CALMING AND BALANCING EFFECT ON THE NERVOUS SYSTEM. DURING THIS TYPE OF MASSAGE, WE USE MAINLY SUCH TYPES OF MASSAGE TECHNIQUES AS STROKING, KNEADING, GLIDING, VIBRATION.
IN SWEDEN, "SWEDISH MASSAGE" IS KNOWN AS A CLASSIC MASSAGE AND THAT IS EXACTLY WHAT IT IS - A CLASSIC TREATMENT THAT REPRESENTS THE WESTERN STANDARD FOR MASSAGE.

SHOULDER AND NECK MASSAGE

DID YOU KNOW THAT HAVING A STRESSFUL JOB AND BEING OVERWORKED COULD HAVE AN IMPACT ON YOUR NECK? YOU JUST CARRY TENSION IN THAT PART OF YOUR BODY. THAT'S WHY A SHOULDER AND NECK MASSAGE IS SO IMPORTANT.
SUCH MASSAGE CAN BRING MANY BENEFITS. FIRST OF ALL, IT CAN HELP REDUCE MIGRAINES AND EYE STRAINS. WE CAN SAY THAT THIS TYPE OF MASSAGE IS A NATURAL ALTERNATIVE FOR PAINKILLERS. SECONDLY, A NECK MASSAGE SESSION HELPS TO REDUCE MUSCULAR TENSION AND EASE DAY-TO-DAY STRESS.
WHAT IS INTERESTING, WE CARRY ANXIETY SYMPTOMS IN OUR SHOULDERS AND NECK. RESEARCH HAS SHOWN THAT WHEN OUR BODY IS RELAXED, SO IS OUR NERVOUS SYSTEM. THAT'S MEAN NOT ONLY YOUR BODY WILL BENEFIT FROM MASSAGES BUT YOUR MOOD ELEVATES TOO!

HOT STONE MASSAGE

This type of massage uses warmed stones, usually basalts, to relax tense muscles, improve blood circulation and even relieve pain. The idea is simple. The stones should be heated to such a temperature that the heat will be gently penetrating the skin to release toxins and create a deeper muscle relaxation than in a standard massage. You might wonder how to heat the stones. It's simple. All you need to do is to place the stones in a saucepan and add enough water to cover them. Then attach a candy thermometer to the inside of the pan to check the temperature of the water. Remove the pan from the stove when the water reaches a temperature between 110F and 125F. Hot stone massage is a very interesting type of massage technique, but remember about one important thing, you must make sure that the temperature of the stones is not too high.

HEAD MASSAGE

DO YOU SUFFER FROM HEADACHES? MAYBE YOU HAVE SOME STRESS PROBLEMS? A HEAD MASSAGE CAN HELP IN DEALING WITH THESE ISSUES. THIS TYPE OF MASSAGE IS VERY HELPFUL IN PROMOTING RELAXATION AND REDUCING STRESS. IT LOWERS BODY PRESSURE, REDUCES TENSION HEADACHE SYMPTOMS AND EVEN PROMOTES HAIR GROWTH. A HEAD MASSAGE TECHNIQUE FOCUSES ON DELIVERING SLOW, GENTLE STROKES ON YOUR HEAD AND WORK UP TO LIGHT CIRCULAR MOTIONS THAT GO ACROSS THE HEAD. ALTHOUGH YOU CAN DO A HEAD MASSAGE WITHOUT IT, I RECOMMENDED USING SOME ESSENTIAL OIL. YOU MAY LIKE THE AROMA AND ADDED BENEFITS OF USING THEM.

FOOT MASSAGE

THESE DAYS WE LIVE IN A HURRY, WE ARE ALWAYS BUSY, THAT'S WHY OUR FEET WORK HARD EVERY DAY. JUST LIKE A NECK, BACK, AND SHOULDERS, FEET CAN ALSO BENEFIT FROM REGULAR MASSAGE SESSIONS. IT CAN HELP SLEEP BETTER AND LEAVE YOU WITH REJUVENATED ENERGY TO BRING TO YOUR DAY. THESE BENEFITS ARE CONNECTED WITH THE BELIEF THAT APPLYING PRESSURE TO MORE THAN 7,000 NERVES IN A FOOT CAN RELEASE ENERGETIC BLOCKAGES IN THE REST OF A BODY. A FOOT MASSAGE IS ALSO VERY USEFUL IF WE WANT TO IMPROVE THE CIRCULATION OF BLOOD AROUND THE BODY. GENERALLY, FOOT MASSAGE SESSIONS ARE PERFORMED USING HANDS, BUT YOU CAN USE SOME EXTRA EQUIPMENT SUCH, AS STICKS OR ROLLERS.

SWEDISH MASSAGE

A SWEDISH MASSAGE IS ONE OF THE MOST POPULAR MASSAGE TECHNIQUE IN THE WESTERN WORLD.
AS THE NAME SUGGESTS, ORIGINALLY IT COMES FROM SWEDEN. IT INVOLVES USING A LOT OF FORCE TO RELIEVE PRESSURE AND PAIN. IT IS A WHOLE-BODY MASSAGE TECHNIQUE THAT HELPS IN RESTORING HEALTH - CREATING A CALMING AND BALANCING EFFECT ON THE NERVOUS SYSTEM. DURING THIS TYPE OF MASSAGE, WE USE MAINLY SUCH TYPES OF MASSAGE TECHNIQUES AS STROKING, KNEADING, GLIDING, VIBRATION.
IN SWEDEN, "SWEDISH MASSAGE" IS KNOWN AS A CLASSIC MASSAGE AND THAT IS EXACTLY WHAT IT IS - A CLASSIC TREATMENT THAT REPRESENTS THE WESTERN STANDARD FOR MASSAGE.

SHOULDER AND NECK MASSAGE

DID YOU KNOW THAT HAVING A STRESSFUL JOB AND BEING OVERWORKED COULD HAVE AN IMPACT ON YOUR NECK? YOU JUST CARRY TENSION IN THAT PART OF YOUR BODY. THAT'S WHY A SHOULDER AND NECK MASSAGE IS SO IMPORTANT.

SUCH MASSAGE CAN BRING MANY BENEFITS. FIRST OF ALL, IT CAN HELP REDUCE MIGRAINES AND EYE STRAINS. WE CAN SAY THAT THIS TYPE OF MASSAGE IS A NATURAL ALTERNATIVE FOR PAINKILLERS. SECONDLY, A NECK MASSAGE SESSION HELPS TO REDUCE MUSCULAR TENSION AND EASE DAY-TO-DAY STRESS.

WHAT IS INTERESTING, WE CARRY ANXIETY SYMPTOMS IN OUR SHOULDERS AND NECK. RESEARCH HAS SHOWN THAT WHEN OUR BODY IS RELAXED, SO IS OUR NERVOUS SYSTEM. THAT'S MEAN NOT ONLY YOUR BODY WILL BENEFIT FROM MASSAGES BUT YOUR MOOD ELEVATES TOO!

HOT STONE MASSAGE

THIS TYPE OF MASSAGE USES WARMED STONES, USUALLY BASALTS, TO RELAX TENSE MUSCLES, IMPROVE BLOOD CIRCULATION AND EVEN RELIEVE PAIN. THE IDEA IS SIMPLE. THE STONES SHOULD BE HEATED TO SUCH A TEMPERATURE THAT THE HEAT WILL BE GENTLY PENETRATING THE SKIN TO RELEASE TOXINS AND CREATE A DEEPER MUSCLE RELAXATION THAN IN A STANDARD MASSAGE. YOU MIGHT WONDER HOW TO HEAT THE STONES. IT'S SIMPLE. ALL YOU NEED TO DO IS TO PLACE THE STONES IN A SAUCEPAN AND ADD ENOUGH WATER TO COVER THEM. THEN ATTACH A CANDY THERMOMETER TO THE INSIDE OF THE PAN TO CHECK THE TEMPERATURE OF THE WATER. REMOVE THE PAN FROM THE STOVE WHEN THE WATER REACHES A TEMPERATURE BETWEEN 110F AND 125F. HOT STONE MASSAGE IS A VERY INTERESTING TYPE OF MASSAGE TECHNIQUE, BUT REMEMBER ABOUT ONE IMPORTANT THING, YOU MUST MAKE SURE THAT THE TEMPERATURE OF THE STONES IS NOT TOO HIGH.

HEAD MASSAGE

DO YOU SUFFER FROM HEADACHES? MAYBE YOU HAVE SOME STRESS PROBLEMS? A HEAD MASSAGE CAN HELP IN DEALING WITH THESE ISSUES. THIS TYPE OF MASSAGE IS VERY HELPFUL IN PROMOTING RELAXATION AND REDUCING STRESS. IT LOWERS BODY PRESSURE, REDUCES TENSION HEADACHE SYMPTOMS AND EVEN PROMOTES HAIR GROWTH. A HEAD MASSAGE TECHNIQUE FOCUSES ON DELIVERING SLOW, GENTLE STROKES ON YOUR HEAD AND WORK UP TO LIGHT CIRCULAR MOTIONS THAT GO ACROSS THE HEAD. ALTHOUGH YOU CAN DO A HEAD MASSAGE WITHOUT IT, I RECOMMENDED USING SOME ESSENTIAL OIL. YOU MAY LIKE THE AROMA AND ADDED BENEFITS OF USING THEM.

FOOT MASSAGE

THESE DAYS WE LIVE IN A HURRY, WE ARE ALWAYS BUSY, THAT'S WHY OUR FEET WORK HARD EVERY DAY. JUST LIKE A NECK, BACK, AND SHOULDERS, FEET CAN ALSO BENEFIT FROM REGULAR MASSAGE SESSIONS. IT CAN HELP SLEEP BETTER AND LEAVE YOU WITH REJUVENATED ENERGY TO BRING TO YOUR DAY. THESE BENEFITS ARE CONNECTED WITH THE BELIEF THAT APPLYING PRESSURE TO MORE THAN 7,000 NERVES IN A FOOT CAN RELEASE ENERGETIC BLOCKAGES IN THE REST OF A BODY. A FOOT MASSAGE IS ALSO VERY USEFUL IF WE WANT TO IMPROVE THE CIRCULATION OF BLOOD AROUND THE BODY. GENERALLY, FOOT MASSAGE SESSIONS ARE PERFORMED USING HANDS, BUT YOU CAN USE SOME EXTRA EQUIPMENT SUCH, AS STICKS OR ROLLERS.

SWEDISH MASSAGE

A SWEDISH MASSAGE IS ONE OF THE MOST POPULAR MASSAGE TECHNIQUE IN THE WESTERN WORLD.
AS THE NAME SUGGESTS, ORIGINALLY IT COMES FROM SWEDEN. IT INVOLVES USING A LOT OF FORCE TO RELIEVE PRESSURE AND PAIN. IT IS A WHOLE-BODY MASSAGE TECHNIQUE THAT HELPS IN RESTORING HEALTH - CREATING A CALMING AND BALANCING EFFECT ON THE NERVOUS SYSTEM. DURING THIS TYPE OF MASSAGE, WE USE MAINLY SUCH TYPES OF MASSAGE TECHNIQUES AS STROKING, KNEADING, GLIDING, VIBRATION.
IN SWEDEN, "SWEDISH MASSAGE" IS KNOWN AS A CLASSIC MASSAGE AND THAT IS EXACTLY WHAT IT IS - A CLASSIC TREATMENT THAT REPRESENTS THE WESTERN STANDARD FOR MASSAGE.

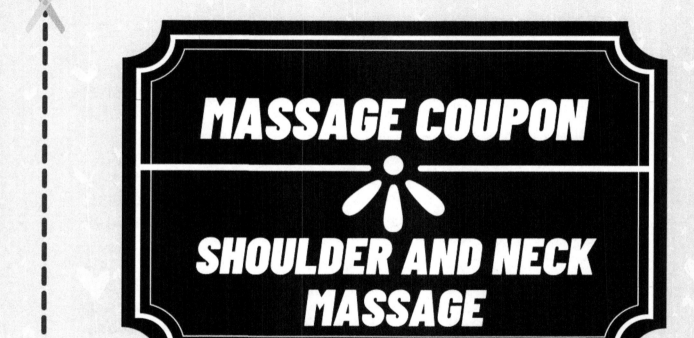

SHOULDER AND NECK MASSAGE

DID YOU KNOW THAT HAVING A STRESSFUL JOB AND BEING OVERWORKED COULD HAVE AN IMPACT ON YOUR NECK? YOU JUST CARRY TENSION IN THAT PART OF YOUR BODY. THAT'S WHY A SHOULDER AND NECK MASSAGE IS SO IMPORTANT.

SUCH MASSAGE CAN BRING MANY BENEFITS. FIRST OF ALL, IT CAN HELP REDUCE MIGRAINES AND EYE STRAINS. WE CAN SAY THAT THIS TYPE OF MASSAGE IS A NATURAL ALTERNATIVE FOR PAINKILLERS. SECONDLY, A NECK MASSAGE SESSION HELPS TO REDUCE MUSCULAR TENSION AND EASE DAY-TO-DAY STRESS.

WHAT IS INTERESTING, WE CARRY ANXIETY SYMPTOMS IN OUR SHOULDERS AND NECK. RESEARCH HAS SHOWN THAT WHEN OUR BODY IS RELAXED, SO IS OUR NERVOUS SYSTEM. THAT'S MEAN NOT ONLY YOUR BODY WILL BENEFIT FROM MASSAGES BUT YOUR MOOD ELEVATES TOO!

HOT STONE MASSAGE

THIS TYPE OF MASSAGE USES WARMED STONES, USUALLY BASALTS, TO RELAX TENSE MUSCLES, IMPROVE BLOOD CIRCULATION AND EVEN RELIEVE PAIN. THE IDEA IS SIMPLE. THE STONES SHOULD BE HEATED TO SUCH A TEMPERATURE THAT THE HEAT WILL BE GENTLY PENETRATING THE SKIN TO RELEASE TOXINS AND CREATE A DEEPER MUSCLE RELAXATION THAN IN A STANDARD MASSAGE. YOU MIGHT WONDER HOW TO HEAT THE STONES. IT'S SIMPLE. ALL YOU NEED TO DO IS TO PLACE THE STONES IN A SAUCEPAN AND ADD ENOUGH WATER TO COVER THEM. THEN ATTACH A CANDY THERMOMETER TO THE INSIDE OF THE PAN TO CHECK THE TEMPERATURE OF THE WATER. REMOVE THE PAN FROM THE STOVE WHEN THE WATER REACHES A TEMPERATURE BETWEEN 110F AND 125F. HOT STONE MASSAGE IS A VERY INTERESTING TYPE OF MASSAGE TECHNIQUE, BUT REMEMBER ABOUT ONE IMPORTANT THING, YOU MUST MAKE SURE THAT THE TEMPERATURE OF THE STONES IS NOT TOO HIGH.

HEAD MASSAGE

Do you suffer from headaches? Maybe you have some stress problems? A head massage can help in dealing with these issues. This type of massage is very helpful in promoting relaxation and reducing stress. It lowers body pressure, reduces tension headache symptoms and even promotes hair growth. A head massage technique focuses on delivering slow, gentle strokes on your head and work up to light circular motions that go across the head. Although you can do a head massage without it, I recommended using some essential oil. You may like the aroma and added benefits of using them.

FOOT MASSAGE

THESE DAYS WE LIVE IN A HURRY, WE ARE ALWAYS BUSY, THAT'S WHY OUR FEET WORK HARD EVERY DAY. JUST LIKE A NECK, BACK, AND SHOULDERS, FEET CAN ALSO BENEFIT FROM REGULAR MASSAGE SESSIONS. IT CAN HELP SLEEP BETTER AND LEAVE YOU WITH REJUVENATED ENERGY TO BRING TO YOUR DAY. THESE BENEFITS ARE CONNECTED WITH THE BELIEF THAT APPLYING PRESSURE TO MORE THAN 7,000 NERVES IN A FOOT CAN RELEASE ENERGETIC BLOCKAGES IN THE REST OF A BODY. A FOOT MASSAGE IS ALSO VERY USEFUL IF WE WANT TO IMPROVE THE CIRCULATION OF BLOOD AROUND THE BODY. GENERALLY, FOOT MASSAGE SESSIONS ARE PERFORMED USING HANDS, BUT YOU CAN USE SOME EXTRA EQUIPMENT SUCH, AS STICKS OR ROLLERS.

SWEDISH MASSAGE

A SWEDISH MASSAGE IS ONE OF THE MOST POPULAR MASSAGE TECHNIQUE IN THE WESTERN WORLD.
AS THE NAME SUGGESTS, ORIGINALLY IT COMES FROM SWEDEN. IT INVOLVES USING A LOT OF FORCE TO RELIEVE PRESSURE AND PAIN. IT IS A WHOLE-BODY MASSAGE TECHNIQUE THAT HELPS IN RESTORING HEALTH - CREATING A CALMING AND BALANCING EFFECT ON THE NERVOUS SYSTEM. DURING THIS TYPE OF MASSAGE, WE USE MAINLY SUCH TYPES OF MASSAGE TECHNIQUES AS STROKING, KNEADING, GLIDING, VIBRATION.
IN SWEDEN, "SWEDISH MASSAGE" IS KNOWN AS A CLASSIC MASSAGE AND THAT IS EXACTLY WHAT IT IS - A CLASSIC TREATMENT THAT REPRESENTS THE WESTERN STANDARD FOR MASSAGE.

SHOULDER AND NECK MASSAGE

Did you know that having a stressful job and being overworked could have an impact on your neck? You just carry tension in that part of your body. That's why a shoulder and neck massage is so important.

Such massage can bring many benefits. First of all, it can help reduce migraines and eye strains. We can say that this type of massage is a natural alternative for painkillers.

Secondly, a neck massage session helps to reduce muscular tension and ease day-to-day stress.

What is interesting, we carry anxiety symptoms in our shoulders and neck. Research has shown that when our body is relaxed, so is our nervous system. That's mean not only your body will benefit from massages but your mood elevates too!

HOT STONE MASSAGE

This type of massage uses warmed stones, usually basalts, to relax tense muscles, improve blood circulation and even relieve pain. The idea is simple. The stones should be heated to such a temperature that the heat will be gently penetrating the skin to release toxins and create a deeper muscle relaxation than in a standard massage. You might wonder how to heat the stones. It's simple. All you need to do is to place the stones in a saucepan and add enough water to cover them. Then attach a candy thermometer to the inside of the pan to check the temperature of the water. Remove the pan from the stove when the water reaches a temperature between 110F and 125F. Hot stone massage is a very interesting type of massage technique, but remember about one important thing, you must make sure that the temperature of the stones is not too high.

HEAD MASSAGE

DO YOU SUFFER FROM HEADACHES? MAYBE YOU HAVE SOME STRESS PROBLEMS? A HEAD MASSAGE CAN HELP IN DEALING WITH THESE ISSUES. THIS TYPE OF MASSAGE IS VERY HELPFUL IN PROMOTING RELAXATION AND REDUCING STRESS. IT LOWERS BODY PRESSURE, REDUCES TENSION HEADACHE SYMPTOMS AND EVEN PROMOTES HAIR GROWTH. A HEAD MASSAGE TECHNIQUE FOCUSES ON DELIVERING SLOW, GENTLE STROKES ON YOUR HEAD AND WORK UP TO LIGHT CIRCULAR MOTIONS THAT GO ACROSS THE HEAD. ALTHOUGH YOU CAN DO A HEAD MASSAGE WITHOUT IT, I RECOMMENDED USING SOME ESSENTIAL OIL. YOU MAY LIKE THE AROMA AND ADDED BENEFITS OF USING THEM.

FOOT MASSAGE

THESE DAYS WE LIVE IN A HURRY, WE ARE ALWAYS BUSY, THAT'S WHY OUR FEET WORK HARD EVERY DAY. JUST LIKE A NECK, BACK, AND SHOULDERS, FEET CAN ALSO BENEFIT FROM REGULAR MASSAGE SESSIONS. IT CAN HELP SLEEP BETTER AND LEAVE YOU WITH REJUVENATED ENERGY TO BRING TO YOUR DAY. THESE BENEFITS ARE CONNECTED WITH THE BELIEF THAT APPLYING PRESSURE TO MORE THAN 7,000 NERVES IN A FOOT CAN RELEASE ENERGETIC BLOCKAGES IN THE REST OF A BODY. A FOOT MASSAGE IS ALSO VERY USEFUL IF WE WANT TO IMPROVE THE CIRCULATION OF BLOOD AROUND THE BODY. GENERALLY, FOOT MASSAGE SESSIONS ARE PERFORMED USING HANDS, BUT YOU CAN USE SOME EXTRA EQUIPMENT SUCH, AS STICKS OR ROLLERS.

SWEDISH MASSAGE

A Swedish massage is one of the most popular massage technique in the western world.
As the name suggests, originally it comes from Sweden. It involves using a lot of force to relieve pressure and pain. It is a whole-body massage technique that helps in restoring health - creating a calming and balancing effect on the nervous system. During this type of massage, we use mainly such types of massage techniques as stroking, kneading, gliding, vibration.
In Sweden, "Swedish massage" is known as a classic massage and that is exactly what it is - a classic treatment that represents the western standard for massage.

SHOULDER AND NECK MASSAGE

DID YOU KNOW THAT HAVING A STRESSFUL JOB AND BEING OVERWORKED COULD HAVE AN IMPACT ON YOUR NECK? YOU JUST CARRY TENSION IN THAT PART OF YOUR BODY. THAT'S WHY A SHOULDER AND NECK MASSAGE IS SO IMPORTANT.

SUCH MASSAGE CAN BRING MANY BENEFITS. FIRST OF ALL, IT CAN HELP REDUCE MIGRAINES AND EYE STRAINS. WE CAN SAY THAT THIS TYPE OF MASSAGE IS A NATURAL ALTERNATIVE FOR PAINKILLERS. SECONDLY, A NECK MASSAGE SESSION HELPS TO REDUCE MUSCULAR TENSION AND EASE DAY-TO-DAY STRESS.

WHAT IS INTERESTING, WE CARRY ANXIETY SYMPTOMS IN OUR SHOULDERS AND NECK. RESEARCH HAS SHOWN THAT WHEN OUR BODY IS RELAXED, SO IS OUR NERVOUS SYSTEM. THAT'S MEAN NOT ONLY YOUR BODY WILL BENEFIT FROM MASSAGES BUT YOUR MOOD ELEVATES TOO!

HOT STONE MASSAGE

This type of massage uses warmed stones, usually basalts, to relax tense muscles, improve blood circulation and even relieve pain. The idea is simple. The stones should be heated to such a temperature that the heat will be gently penetrating the skin to release toxins and create a deeper muscle relaxation than in a standard massage. You might wonder how to heat the stones. It's simple. All you need to do is to place the stones in a saucepan and add enough water to cover them. Then attach a candy thermometer to the inside of the pan to check the temperature of the water. Remove the pan from the stove when the water reaches a temperature between 110F and 125F. Hot stone massage is a very interesting type of massage technique, but remember about one important thing, you must make sure that the temperature of the stones is not too high.

Printed in Great Britain
by Amazon